Cryptocurrency Guide For Beginners

By

Ryan Rodrigues Souza

Copyright © 2024 Ryan Rodrigues Souza.
All rights reserved.

No part of this publication may be reproduced, distributed, or transmitted in any form or by any means, including photocopying, recording, or other electronic or mechanical methods, without the prior written permission of the publisher, except in the case of brief quotations embodied in critical reviews and certain other noncommercial uses permitted by copyright law.

Disclaimer

The information provided in this book is for general informational purposes only and should not be considered as investment advice. Cryptocurrency investments are risky and may result in significant losses.

TABLE OF CONTENT

INTRODUCTION
What is Cryptocurrency?
The History of Money
Evolution to Digital Currencies
Key Milestones in Cryptocurrency History
Importance of Cryptocurrencies

CHAPTER ONE
Understanding Blockchain Technology
- Fundamentals of Blockchain
- How Blockchain Works
- Applications of Blockchain Beyond Cryptocurrencies

CHAPTER TWO
Major Cryptocurrencies
- Bitcoin (BTC)
- Ethereum (ETH)
- Other Notable Cryptocurrencies

CHAPTER THREE
Acquiring and Storing Cryptocurrencies
- Buying Cryptocurrencies
- Storing Cryptocurrencies

CHAPTER FOUR
Using Cryptocurrencies
- Making Transactions
- Everyday Use of Cryptocurrencies
- Investing in Cryptocurrencies

CHAPTER FIVE
Security and scams in crypto currency
- Common Security Risks
- Hacking, Phishing, and Malware
- Recognizing and Avoiding Scams
- Regulation and legal issues

CHAPTER SIX
Advanced Topics in Cryptocurrency
- Mining and Proof-of-Work
- Smart Contracts and DApps
- Case Studies and Real-World Examples
- Businesses and Industries Using Blockchain

CHAPTER SEVEN
Resources and Further Reading
- Online Resources

CONCLUSION

Appendix A: Glossary of Terms
Appendix B: Frequently Asked Questions (FAQ)
Appendix C: Useful Tools and Software

INTRODUCTION

Cryptocurrencies have sparked a transformative change in both finance and digital technology. Essentially, these are decentralized digital assets secured by cryptography, making them resistant to counterfeiting and double-spending. Unlike traditional currencies, which are issued by governments and regulated by central banks, cryptocurrencies function on decentralized networks using blockchain technology. This key distinction provides several benefits, including greater transparency, reduced risk of fraud, and the removal of intermediaries in financial transactions.

The emergence of cryptocurrencies stands as one of the most impactful financial innovations of the 21st century. Initially adopted by a small group of technologists and libertarians, they have since gained significant attention from investors, businesses, and regulatory bodies worldwide. Today, cryptocurrencies such as Bitcoin and Ethereum are recognized not only as speculative assets but also as viable alternatives to conventional financial systems. This growing acceptance suggests a potential shift in our understanding of money, ownership, and economic value.

What is Cryptocurrency?

A cryptocurrency is a type of digital or virtual currency that utilizes cryptographic methods to secure transactions, manage the creation of new units, and validate the transfer of assets. The primary characteristic of a cryptocurrency is its decentralized structure, usually implemented via blockchain technology, a distributed ledger maintained by a network of computers, or nodes. Unlike traditional currencies that are issued by central banks, cryptocurrencies are often generated through a process known as mining, which involves solving intricate mathematical problems to add new transactions to the blockchain.

Bitcoin, launched in 2009 by an anonymous figure named Satoshi Nakamoto, was the first cryptocurrency and continues to be the most prominent and valuable. Its introduction marked the dawn of a new era in digital finance, where trust is established not by centralized entities but through decentralized networks and cryptographic verification. Other well-known cryptocurrencies include Ethereum, which pioneered smart contracts, and numerous altcoins that serve various functions, from payment systems to platform tokens for decentralized applications (DApps).

The History of Money

To grasp the importance of cryptocurrencies, it is crucial to delve into the history of money. Throughout human history, money has undergone various transformations, from barter systems to commodity money (like gold and silver) and eventually to fiat money currencies that lack intrinsic value but are recognized as money by government regulation. Money's primary roles include acting as a medium of exchange, a unit of account, and a store of value.

The development of money has consistently been driven by the quest for more efficient, secure, and reliable systems. The shift from barter to commodity money resolved the inefficiencies of direct exchanges, while fiat money, backed by legal frameworks and central banks, offered greater flexibility and control over economic policies. Nonetheless, fiat money systems are not without issues, such as inflation, counterfeiting, and dependence on centralized institutions, which can sometimes fail or behave in ways that undermine public trust.

Evolution to Digital Currencies

The idea of digital currencies has roots in the late 20th century when efforts were made to create electronic cash systems. One of the earliest examples was DigiCash, established by cryptographer David Chaum in the late 1980s. DigiCash sought to create a form of digital money that could be transferred anonymously, but it ultimately failed due to insufficient adoption and lack of support from financial institutions. Other early digital currency projects, such as e-gold and Liberty Reserve, also faced regulatory hurdles and were eventually shut down.

The breakthrough for digital currencies occurred with the introduction of blockchain technology, exemplified by Bitcoin. Blockchain technology enabled the achievement of decentralized consensus without the need for a central authority. This innovation tackled the double-spending problem where digital money could be duplicated and spent multiple times by ensuring all transactions are recorded in a tamper-proof ledger distributed across the entire network. This decentralized model provided a level of security and trust that previous digital currency systems lacked.

Key Milestones in Cryptocurrency History

The development of cryptocurrency has been shaped by pivotal moments that have defined its evolution and acceptance. Bitcoin's launch in 2009 marked a groundbreaking milestone, proving the feasibility of a decentralized digital currency.

A significant event followed in 2010 when programmer Laszlo Hanyecz conducted the first real-world Bitcoin transaction, purchasing two pizzas for 10,000 Bitcoins, an occasion now commemorated annually as Bitcoin Pizza Day.

The introduction of Ethereum in 2015 introduced a revolutionary concept with smart contracts, enabling agreements to be encoded directly into code and self-executed. Ethereum's platform facilitated the creation of decentralized applications (DApps), broadening the potential applications of cryptocurrencies beyond simple transactions.

Another notable milestone was the Initial Coin Offering (ICO) boom in 2017, where numerous projects raised substantial funds through token sales.

While this period fueled innovation and investment, it also brought forth challenges such as fraudulent activities and increased regulatory scrutiny. More recently, the emergence of decentralized finance (DeFi) and non-fungible tokens (NFTs) has showcased the ongoing evolution and expanding impact of cryptocurrencies across industries like finance, art, and entertainment.

Importance of Cryptocurrencies

Cryptocurrencies offer several compelling advantages that underscore their relevance and significance in today's digital economy. Firstly, they present an alternative to traditional financial systems that may be inaccessible or inefficient for many people globally.

By enabling peer-to-peer transactions without intermediaries, cryptocurrencies reduce costs and enhance transaction speeds, particularly beneficial in regions with limited financial access or underdeveloped infrastructure.

Furthermore, cryptocurrencies promote financial inclusion by granting the unbanked and underbanked populations access to financial services.

With just a smartphone and internet connection, individuals can securely save, send, and receive money, facilitating participation in the global economy. Additionally, the transparency and immutability of blockchain transactions provide heightened security and trust, addressing issues like corruption and fraud prevalent in traditional financial systems.

Cryptocurrencies signify a profound shift in the perception and utilization of money. Leveraging blockchain technology, they offer a decentralized, secure, and efficient alternative to conventional financial systems. As the world increasingly embraces digital transformation, cryptocurrencies are poised for continued growth and adoption, potentially revolutionizing sectors ranging from banking and commerce to investment and governance.

Despite existing challenges such as regulatory complexities and technological constraints, the transformative potential of cryptocurrencies in democratizing finance and fostering innovation remains undeniable, marking them a pivotal area for ongoing study and advancement.

CHAPTER ONE

Understanding Blockchain Technology

Blockchain technology has garnered significant attention not only for its role in cryptocurrencies but also for its potential to revolutionize various industries. Essentially, blockchain is a decentralized digital ledger distributed across multiple computers, ensuring that recorded transactions cannot be altered retroactively. This immutability and transparency make blockchain highly secure and reliable. Initially developed for Bitcoin, blockchain now supports diverse applications from supply chain management to healthcare.

To comprehend blockchain technology involves exploring its foundational principles, operational mechanics, types, and broad applications. At its core, blockchain establishes trust in a trustless environment, eliminating the need for intermediaries and offering efficiency, cost reduction, and enhanced security across industries. As blockchain continues to evolve and integrate into mainstream applications, its transformative potential becomes increasingly apparent.

Fundamentals of Blockchain

The fundamentals of blockchain technology lie in its architecture and core principles. A blockchain consists of blocks linked in chronological order, each containing transaction data, a timestamp, and a cryptographic hash of the previous block. This cryptographic linkage ensures data integrity and security, making it extremely difficult to alter any information without affecting the entire chain.

Decentralization is key to blockchain's operation. Unlike centralized databases managed by a single entity, blockchain operates on a peer-to-peer network of computers (nodes). Each node maintains a copy of the blockchain and participates in consensus mechanisms like Proof of Work (PoW) or Proof of Stake (PoS). These mechanisms validate transactions and maintain the integrity of the blockchain, ensuring agreement among all participants.

How Blockchain Works

Blockchain functions through cryptographic techniques, consensus protocols, and decentralized networking. When a new transaction is initiated, it is broadcast to the network where nodes validate it based on consensus rules. In Bitcoin's Proof of Work system, miners compete to solve complex puzzles, with the first to solve it adding a new block to the chain and receiving rewards. This process, known as mining, ensures transaction verification and adds blocks to the blockchain.

Once added, blocks are distributed to all nodes, updating their copies of the blockchain. Blockchain's immutability stems from cryptographic hashing and block chaining, where altering any block would disrupt subsequent blocks, alerting the network. This security feature ensures that blockchain data remains tamper-proof and secure.

Types of Blockchains

Blockchains are categorized into public, private, and consortium types, each with unique characteristics and applications:

I. **Public Blockchains:** Open to anyone, public blockchains like Bitcoin and Ethereum are fully decentralized. They offer high security and transparency but may be slower due to extensive computational needs.

II. **Private Blockchains:** Restricted to specific participants, private blockchains offer greater control and efficiency but sacrifice some transparency and decentralization. They are common in enterprise settings.

III. **Consortium Blockchains:** Managed by a group of organizations, consortium blockchains strike a balance between decentralization and control. They are efficient and scalable, ideal for collaborative industries.

Understanding these blockchain types helps determine their suitability for different use cases, from global financial transactions to private enterprise applications.

Applications of Blockchain Beyond Cryptocurrencies

While blockchain technology is most famous as the backbone of cryptocurrencies like Bitcoin and Ethereum, its utility extends well beyond digital money. Blockchain's decentralization, transparency, and immutability make it suitable for diverse industries and purposes.

I. **Supply Chain Management:** Blockchain enhances transparency and traceability in supply chains by maintaining an unchangeable record of transactions from product origin to delivery. This helps prevent fraud, ensures product authenticity, and boosts overall efficiency. Companies such as Walmart and IBM use blockchain to monitor food safety and reduce risks of contamination.

II. **Healthcare:** In healthcare, blockchain securely stores and shares patient records, ensuring accuracy, timeliness, and limited access to authorized parties. This improves patient care, cuts administrative costs, and strengthens data security. Blockchain also aids in managing pharmaceutical supply chains

to combat counterfeit drugs and ensure the integrity of medical products.
III. **Voting Systems:** Blockchain offers secure, transparent, and tamper-proof voting systems by recording votes on an immutable ledger. This safeguards election results and builds trust in democratic processes. Pilot projects worldwide explore blockchain's potential in revolutionizing voting systems.
IV. **Real Estate:** Blockchain simplifies property transactions by providing a transparent, secure method for recording transactions. Smart contracts automate and enforce agreements, reducing fraud and eliminating intermediaries. Blockchain-based property registries streamline ownership transfers and enhance accuracy in property records.
V. **Finance and Banking:** Beyond cryptocurrencies, blockchain revolutionizes finance by enabling faster, secure, and cost-effective transactions. It reduces intermediaries in cross-border payments, enhancing speed and lowering costs. Smart contracts automate complex financial agreements like derivatives and insurance, boosting efficiency and cutting operational risks.

Blockchain's transformative potential spans beyond its origin in cryptocurrencies, addressing inefficiencies and vulnerabilities in traditional systems. As businesses and governments adopt blockchain solutions, the technology promises significant advancements in supply chain management, healthcare, voting systems, real estate, and finance. Understanding blockchain and its diverse applications is crucial in navigating the evolving digital landscape.

CHAPTER TWO

Major Cryptocurrencies

P
Cryptocurrencies have become integral to the financial landscape, boasting hundreds of coins and tokens available today. Among these, several stand out due to their market capitalization, technological advancements, and widespread adoption. These major cryptocurrencies not only spearheaded the digital currency realm but also continue to influence significant trends and developments in the blockchain industry. Understanding these leading cryptocurrencies is crucial for comprehending the broader ecosystem, offering insights into current dynamics and future trajectories in digital finance.

Bitcoin (BTC) and Ethereum (ETH) represent the foremost cryptocurrencies, each renowned for distinct attributes and functionalities. Often likened to digital gold, Bitcoin features a finite supply and serves as a store of value, whereas Ethereum is celebrated for its smart contract capabilities, facilitating decentralized applications (DApps) and intricate financial instruments.

Alongside Bitcoin and Ethereum, notable cryptocurrencies such as Litecoin, Ripple, Bitcoin Cash, and Cardano have emerged, each addressing specific needs and challenges within the digital currency space. This section delves into these major cryptocurrencies, exploring their histories, technical intricacies, and practical applications.

Bitcoin (BTC)

Bitcoin, introduced in 2009 by the anonymous Satoshi Nakamoto, marked the genesis of cryptocurrencies with the publication of the white paper "Bitcoin: A Peer-to-Peer Electronic Cash System." The creation of Bitcoin aimed to establish a decentralized financial system immune to double-spending issues without relying on a trusted intermediary.

Initially embraced by a niche community, Bitcoin gained traction with notable milestones such as the first recorded transaction of 10,000 BTC for two pizzas in 2010, celebrated annually as Bitcoin Pizza Day. Over time, Bitcoin garnered mainstream attention through price surges and media coverage, solidifying its position as the dominant cryptocurrency by market capitalization despite regulatory challenges and market fluctuations.

Technical Aspects

Bitcoin operates on a decentralized network using Proof of Work (PoW) consensus. Miners compete to solve complex puzzles, securing the network and validating transactions by adding blocks to the blockchain. This mining process demands substantial computational resources and energy consumption.

Secured by cryptographic hashes linking each block, Bitcoin's blockchain ensures data integrity and immutability. Transactions are pseudonymous, with transaction details visible publicly while the identities of users remain obfuscated. With a fixed supply of 21 million coins, Bitcoin is considered a deflationary asset akin to gold, bolstering its appeal as a store of value.

Use Cases and Adoption

Bitcoin primarily serves as a digital store of value and an alternative to fiat currencies. Investors view Bitcoin as a hedge against inflation and economic uncertainty, attracted by its decentralized nature and predictable supply. Moreover, Bitcoin facilitates remittances and cross-border transactions, offering faster and cheaper alternatives to traditional banking systems.

Adoption of Bitcoin is expanding, with increasing numbers of merchants accepting it as payment. Major corporations like Microsoft and AT&T now embrace Bitcoin, while financial institutions offer related services. Infrastructure developments such as wallets and exchanges have streamlined Bitcoin transactions. Additionally, Bitcoin's pioneering role has spurred the creation of financial products like futures and ETFs, integrating it further into traditional financial markets.

Ethereum (ETH)

Ethereum, launched in 2015 under Vitalik Buterin's leadership, introduced a revolutionary feature to cryptocurrencies: smart contracts. Unlike Bitcoin, Ethereum functions as a decentralized platform enabling developers to construct and deploy smart contracts and decentralized applications (DApps). Smart contracts are self-executing agreements with terms coded directly into their logic. They automate the execution of agreements once predefined conditions are met, eliminating intermediaries.

The Ethereum platform operates using its native cryptocurrency, Ether (ETH), essential for conducting transactions and executing smart contracts. Developers pay transaction fees, known as "gas," in Ether to run applications and process transactions on the Ethereum network. This fee mechanism incentivizes miners to validate transactions and maintain network security and functionality.

Ethereum Network and Its Applications

The Ethereum network serves as the basis for a broad spectrum of decentralized applications spanning finance, gaming, supply chain management, and more. A significant breakthrough on Ethereum is the emergence of decentralized finance (DeFi) platforms. DeFi encompasses financial services built on blockchain, operating without traditional intermediaries like banks. These services include lending, borrowing, trading, and earning interest on crypto assets.

Ethereum's adaptability has led to the creation of various tokens and standards, such as ERC-20 for fungible tokens and ERC-721 for non-fungible tokens (NFTs). NFTs have gained popularity for trading unique digital assets like art, collectibles, and virtual real estate. Ethereum's capability to support a diverse ecosystem of DApps and tokens positions it as a frontrunner in blockchain innovation.

Key Projects & Decentralized Finance (DeFi)

Numerous projects within the Ethereum ecosystem drive the expansion and adoption of decentralized finance. Noteworthy among these is Uniswap, a decentralized exchange (DEX) enabling direct wallet-to-wallet token trading without centralized intermediaries. MakerDAO is another significant platform within DeFi, facilitating the creation and management of DAI, a stablecoin pegged to the US dollar.

Additional prominent DeFi platforms include Compound and Aave, offering decentralized lending and borrowing services. Users can earn interest on their crypto assets or obtain loans without traditional credit checks, facilitated by smart contract automation. This approach enhances accessibility and efficiency compared to conventional financial services.

The rise of DeFi has fostered yield farming and liquidity mining, where users provide liquidity to DeFi platforms in exchange for rewards. These innovations create opportunities for generating passive income in the crypto sector, boosting interest and engagement within the Ethereum ecosystem.

Other Notable Cryptocurrencies

Litecoin (LTC)

Litecoin, introduced by Charlie Lee in 2011, is often likened to "silver to Bitcoin's gold." It was designed to offer faster transaction times and lower fees compared to Bitcoin by implementing a 2.5-minute block generation time and a different hashing algorithm known as Scrypt. Despite similarities with Bitcoin in its role as a digital currency and store of value, Litecoin's technical adjustments make it more suited for everyday transactions.

Ripple (XRP)

Launched in 2012 by Ripple Labs, Ripple focuses on facilitating fast and cost-effective international payments. Unlike most cryptocurrencies, Ripple prioritizes efficiency in cross-border transactions over decentralization. Its native cryptocurrency, XRP, acts as a bridge currency in its payment protocol, enabling swift transfers between different fiat currencies. Ripple has established partnerships with numerous financial institutions and payment providers, cementing XRP's role in global payments.

Bitcoin Cash (BCH)

Bitcoin Cash emerged in 2017 through a hard fork from Bitcoin aimed at increasing the block size limit to enhance scalability. Advocates argue that BCH's larger blocks allow for more transactions per second at lower fees, making it more suitable for everyday transactions. Despite its contentious inception, Bitcoin Cash has gained prominence and a growing user base in the cryptocurrency community.

Cardano (ADA)

Founded by Charles Hoskinson in 2017, Cardano focuses on sustainability, scalability, and interoperability in blockchain technology. It employs a research-driven approach to development and utilizes the Ouroboros Proof of Stake protocol, designed for energy efficiency compared to Bitcoin's Proof of Work. ADA, Cardano's native cryptocurrency, powers the network and facilitates transactions, aiming to support the creation of smart contracts and decentralized applications addressing real-world challenges.

Overview and Distinctive Features

Each of these notable cryptocurrencies brings distinct innovations catering to specific needs and applications. Litecoin offers faster transactions and lower fees suitable for daily use, while Ripple specializes in efficient international payments for financial institutions. Bitcoin Cash enhances scalability with larger blocks for increased transaction throughput, and Cardano emphasizes sustainability and advanced blockchain research to support robust decentralized applications.

These cryptocurrencies collectively challenge traditional financial systems, emphasizing decentralization and empowering users with greater control over their finances. They drive innovation in blockchain technology across various sectors, including finance, technology, and governance. As the cryptocurrency ecosystem evolves, these major cryptocurrencies are poised to continue shaping the future of digital finance and decentralized applications.

Beyond these major cryptocurrencies, the broader landscape includes thousands of other tokens and coins, each contributing unique features and serving distinct communities and use cases.

Whether privacy-focused, platform-specific, or utility-oriented, the diversity within the cryptocurrency ecosystem highlights the versatility and ongoing innovation in blockchain technology.

As market dynamics and regulatory environments evolve, the landscape of major cryptocurrencies may shift. New projects will emerge while existing ones adapt to meet evolving demands and regulatory challenges.

Regardless of market fluctuations, the foundational principles of decentralization, transparency, and trustless transactions will remain fundamental to the advancement of digital currencies. Understanding these major cryptocurrencies and their unique attributes is essential for stakeholders navigating the dynamic and transformative realm of cryptocurrency.

CHAPTER THREE

Acquiring and Storing Cryptocurrencies

Acquiring and securely storing cryptocurrencies are essential elements for anyone involved in the digital currency ecosystem, whether as a long-term investor or an active trader. This chapter delves into the various methods available for purchasing cryptocurrencies, including centralized exchanges, decentralized exchanges (DEXs), and peer-to-peer marketplaces, while emphasizing best practices for safeguarding digital assets.

Buying Cryptocurrencies

Centralized Exchanges

Centralized exchanges serve as the predominant platforms for buying and selling cryptocurrencies due to their user-friendly interfaces and broad range of trading pairs. These exchanges act as intermediaries, facilitating transactions between buyers and sellers. Users typically register accounts, deposit fiat currencies or other cryptocurrencies, and execute trades through features like market orders and limit orders. Popular centralized exchanges such as Coinbase, Binance, and Kraken offer high liquidity but require users to undergo Know Your Customer (KYC) verification to comply with regulatory standards. Despite their convenience, centralized exchanges pose security risks since users entrust their private keys to the exchange, exposing them to potential hacks and breaches.

Decentralized Exchanges

Decentralized exchanges (DEXs) operate without a central authority, allowing users to trade directly with each other using smart contracts. DEXs enhance security by enabling users to maintain control over their private keys and assets throughout transactions, thereby reducing the risk associated with centralized exchanges. Platforms like Uniswap, SushiSwap, and PancakeSwap, built on Ethereum and other blockchains, enable users to connect their wallets and trade without creating accounts or undergoing KYC procedures. However, DEXs may suffer from lower liquidity and higher transaction fees compared to centralized counterparts. They also require users to be familiar with cryptocurrency wallets and blockchain operations for optimal use.

Trading Platforms and Peer-to-Peer Marketplaces

Beyond exchanges, trading platforms and peer-to-peer marketplaces offer alternatives for buying and selling cryptocurrencies directly from individuals. Platforms such as LocalBitcoins and Paxful facilitate peer-to-peer trading where users negotiate transactions and choose payment methods like bank transfers or digital wallets. This approach provides flexibility and privacy but carries risks such as potential fraud. Users should exercise caution, conduct thorough research on trading partners, and utilize escrow services and dispute resolution mechanisms offered by these platforms to mitigate risks effectively.

Understanding these methods for acquiring cryptocurrencies and implementing secure storage practices is crucial for navigating the evolving landscape of digital finance. Whether opting for centralized exchanges for liquidity and convenience, exploring decentralized alternatives for enhanced security and privacy, or engaging in peer-to-peer transactions for flexibility, users play a pivotal role in safeguarding their digital assets amidst the dynamic and innovative cryptocurrency environment.

Storing Cryptocurrencies

Hot Wallets vs. Cold Wallets

Once you have acquired cryptocurrencies, it is crucial to store them securely to protect against theft, loss, or unauthorized access. Cryptocurrency wallets come in two main types: hot wallets and cold wallets. Hot wallets are connected to the internet and are suitable for storing smaller amounts of cryptocurrencies for everyday transactions and easy access. Examples include mobile wallets, desktop wallets, and web wallets.

On the other hand, cold wallets are offline devices or paper wallets designed for long-term storage and maximum security. Cold wallets store private keys offline, away from potential cyber threats such as hacking and malware. Popular choices for cold storage include hardware wallets like Ledger and Trezor, which offer robust security features and user-friendly interfaces. Paper wallets, where private keys and addresses are printed on paper, are also favored by some users for their simplicity and accessibility.

Security Best Practices

Regardless of the type of wallet chosen, adhering to security best practices is essential to protect your cryptocurrencies. This includes securing private keys and passwords, enabling two-factor authentication (2FA) whenever possible, and keeping wallet software and devices updated with the latest security patches. It is advisable to use strong, unique passwords and refrain from sharing sensitive information online or with third parties.

Furthermore, users should be vigilant against phishing attacks, scams, and malicious software targeting cryptocurrency holders. Always verify the legitimacy of websites and applications before entering sensitive data, and exercise caution with unsolicited messages or requests for personal information. Staying informed about common security threats and developments in cybersecurity is crucial for safeguarding digital assets effectively.

Backup and Recovery

Lastly, having a backup and recovery plan is critical to ensure access to cryptocurrencies in case of loss, theft, or hardware failure. Most cryptocurrency wallets offer backup options like seed phrases or recovery phrases, which can restore access to funds if a device is lost or damaged. Store backup phrases securely in multiple locations, such as a safe deposit box or encrypted digital storage, and avoid keeping them electronically or in easily accessible places.

Acquiring and securely storing cryptocurrencies requires careful planning and proactive security measures to safeguard digital assets. By understanding the different wallet options and implementing best practices for storage and security, individuals can confidently engage in the cryptocurrency ecosystem and leverage the potential of digital finance. As cryptocurrency adoption grows, educating oneself about these essential aspects of ownership becomes increasingly important for navigating the evolving landscape of digital currencies and blockchain technology.

CHAPTER FOUR

Using Cryptocurrencies

Cryptocurrencies provide a decentralized and flexible method for conducting transactions, investing, and participating in the digital economy. Mastering the effective use of cryptocurrencies is crucial for individuals seeking to capitalize on the advantages of digital finance. This chapter explains the various aspects of utilizing cryptocurrencies, including transaction processes, everyday applications, and investment strategies.

Making Transactions

Sending and Receiving Cryptocurrencies

Executing transactions with cryptocurrencies entails transferring digital assets across a blockchain network. To initiate a transfer, users require the recipient's wallet address, a unique alphanumeric identifier linked to their wallet. Users input this address, specify the amount to send, and validate the transaction using their private key.

Transactions are then propagated throughout the network, verified by miners, and permanently recorded on the blockchain, ensuring transparency and security.

Receiving cryptocurrencies involves sharing one's wallet address with the sender. Upon completion of a transaction, users can review transaction details via a blockchain explorer and monitor the status of incoming funds. Cryptocurrency transactions provide swift and secure transfers, with confirmation times varying based on network traffic and transaction fees.

Transaction Fees and Processing Times

When using cryptocurrencies for transactions, understanding transaction fees and processing times is crucial. Transaction fees fluctuate depending on network congestion, transaction size, and chosen fee structure. Higher fees generally expedite confirmation, as miners prioritize transactions offering higher fees for inclusion in upcoming blocks.

Processing times for cryptocurrency transactions span from a few seconds to several minutes or longer, contingent on blockchain network conditions and congestion levels.

Bitcoin transactions, for instance, may encounter prolonged confirmation periods during peak demand, whereas networks like Ethereum and Litecoin often afford quicker transaction speeds.

Everyday Use of Cryptocurrencies

Cryptocurrencies are gaining traction as a viable payment option accepted by merchants worldwide. Leading companies like Microsoft, Overstock, and Shopify now embrace cryptocurrencies for transactions, broadening the utility of digital assets. Dedicated platforms such as BitPay and Coinbase Commerce facilitate seamless integration of cryptocurrency payments into existing checkout systems. This integration not only expands customer payment choices but also reduces transaction fees for merchants.

Payment gateways and point-of-sale (POS) systems streamline cryptocurrency transactions for merchants, seamlessly integrating with their operational frameworks. These solutions empower merchants to securely accept cryptocurrencies, convert them to traditional fiat currency as needed, and efficiently manage transactions.

Platforms like CoinGate and CoinPayments support diverse cryptocurrencies and provide plugins and APIs for easy integration with popular e-commerce platforms.

Investing in Cryptocurrencies

Investment Strategies (HODLing, Trading, Staking)

Investing in cryptocurrencies offers opportunities through varied strategies such as long-term holding (HODLing), trading, and staking. HODLing involves purchasing and retaining cryptocurrencies over extended periods, anticipating their appreciation as an asset class over time. Trading entails short-term buying and selling to profit from price volatility, employing techniques like technical analysis and market trends. Staking involves validating and securing blockchain networks by holding cryptocurrency, earning rewards in return, particularly prominent with proof-of-stake (PoS) systems.

Risks and Rewards

Cryptocurrency investments present both potential rewards and risks due to their volatile nature. Market values can rapidly fluctuate due to factors like market sentiment, regulatory shifts, and technological advancements. While investments can yield substantial returns, they also pose risks of significant losses during market downturns or unforeseen events. Investors are advised to conduct comprehensive research, diversify portfolios, and exercise caution to navigate the unpredictable cryptocurrency landscape effectively.

Regulatory Compliance and Tax Considerations

Investors must navigate varying regulatory landscapes and tax implications associated with cryptocurrency investments. Regulatory approaches differ globally, with some jurisdictions embracing cryptocurrencies while others enforce stringent regulations. Investors should familiarize themselves with local laws, comply with reporting requirements, and fulfill tax obligations related to cryptocurrency transactions. Taxation typically involves capital gains tax calculations based on factors like asset ownership duration and jurisdiction-specific tax regulations.

Using cryptocurrencies offers versatile opportunities for transactions, daily applications, and investment strategies within the digital economy. Whether for peer-to-peer transfers, online shopping, or portfolio diversification, cryptocurrencies provide efficient, decentralized avenues for participating in the digital financial ecosystem. Understanding the nuances of cryptocurrency use, including transaction mechanisms, everyday applications, and investment strategies, empowers individuals to leverage digital finance effectively amidst the evolving landscape of blockchain technology.

CHAPTER FIVE

Security and scams in crypto currency

Cryptocurrencies, due to their decentralized and digital nature, come with unique security challenges and risks. While they offer new financial opportunities, they also attract malicious actors. This chapter explores common security risks, best practices for protecting your assets, and the global regulatory landscape and legal considerations.

Common Security Risks

Hacking, Phishing, and Malware

Hacking is a major threat in the cryptocurrency world, targeting both individuals and exchanges. Hackers use techniques like exploiting software vulnerabilities, social engineering, and brute-force attacks to gain unauthorized access to wallets and exchange accounts.

Phishing attacks deceive users into revealing private keys, passwords, or other sensitive information by posing as legitimate entities. These attacks often occur via fake emails, websites, or malicious links that mimic real cryptocurrency services.

Malware, such as keyloggers and remote access trojans (RATs), can infect devices, allowing hackers to monitor keystrokes, capture screenshots, and control the device, leading to the theft of private keys and access to wallets.

Security Breaches in Exchanges and Wallets

Exchanges and wallets are prime targets for cybercriminals because of the large amounts of cryptocurrency they hold. Security breaches in exchanges can result in significant losses, as seen in high-profile cases like Mt. Gox and Coincheck, where millions of dollars were stolen.

Wallets, especially online and mobile ones, are also vulnerable. Although hardware wallets offer more security by keeping private keys offline, they are still susceptible to physical theft or sophisticated attacks.

Best Practices for Securing Your Assets

To protect your cryptocurrencies, follow these best practices:

Use Strong, Unique Passwords: Create complex passwords for your exchange and wallet accounts and avoid reusing passwords across multiple services.

Enable Two-Factor Authentication (2FA): Add an extra layer of security by enabling 2FA on your accounts. Use apps like Google Authenticator or Authy instead of SMS-based 2FA.

Keep Private Keys Offline:Use hardware or paper wallets to store private keys offline, reducing the risk of online attacks.

Update Software Regularly: Ensure your wallet software, exchange apps, and devices are up to date with the latest security patches.

Secure Your Devices:Use antivirus software, enable firewalls, and avoid downloading unknown files or clicking on suspicious links.

Backup Your Wallet:Create multiple backups of your wallet's recovery phrases or private keys and store them in secure, separate locations.

Recognizing and Avoiding Scams

Scams are common in the cryptocurrency space, with fraudsters constantly devising new schemes. Common scams include:

Ponzi Schemes: Fraudulent investment schemes promising high returns with little risk. They pay returns to earlier investors using funds from new investors.

Fake ICOs: Scammers create fake initial coin offerings to raise funds from investors and then disappear with the money.

Pump and Dump Schemes: Coordinated efforts to inflate a cryptocurrency's price through misleading information, allowing scammers to sell at a profit before the price crashes.

Phishing Scams: Fraudulent communications designed to trick users into revealing private keys or passwords.

To avoid scams, thoroughly research any investment opportunity, verify the legitimacy of the project and its team, and be wary of offers that seem too good to be true. Use reputable sources and platforms, and always double-check URLs and email addresses before entering sensitive information.

Regulation and legal issues

The regulatory landscape for cryptocurrencies varies significantly across different countries. While some countries support cryptocurrencies and blockchain technology, others impose strict regulations or bans. Key regulatory approaches include:

Supportive Regulation: Countries like Switzerland and Singapore have clear regulatory frameworks to support cryptocurrency innovation while ensuring compliance with anti-money laundering (AML) and counter-terrorism financing (CTF) laws.

Cautious Regulation: The United States, European Union, and Canada have a more cautious approach, implementing regulations to protect consumers and prevent illegal activities without stifling innovation.

Restrictive Regulation: Countries such as China and India have imposed stringent regulations or bans on cryptocurrency trading and ICOs to control financial markets and prevent capital flight.

As the cryptocurrency market evolves, regulatory frameworks continue to develop, impacting how users and businesses operate within different jurisdictions.

Legal Considerations for Users and Businesses

Users and businesses must navigate various legal considerations when dealing with cryptocurrencies:

Taxation: Many countries treat cryptocurrencies as taxable assets. Users must report gains and losses from transactions and comply with tax obligations, which can vary based on the type and duration of holding.

Compliance: Businesses dealing in cryptocurrencies must adhere to AML and CTF regulations, implementing KYC procedures to verify customer identities and report suspicious activities.

Consumer Protection: Regulatory bodies may impose requirements to protect consumers, such as ensuring transparency, security, and fair practices in cryptocurrency services.

Intellectual Property: Businesses developing blockchain technology and cryptocurrencies must navigate intellectual property laws to protect their innovations and avoid infringing on existing patents.

Understanding the regulatory landscape and legal considerations is crucial for both users and businesses to ensure compliance and mitigate legal risks. security and scams in the cryptocurrency space present significant challenges that require vigilance and proactive measures.

By understanding common security risks, implementing best practices to protect assets, recognizing and avoiding scams, and staying informed about the regulatory landscape, individuals and businesses can navigate the cryptocurrency ecosystem safely and responsibly. As the industry continues to evolve, ongoing education and awareness are essential to safeguarding digital assets and ensuring a secure and compliant participation in the cryptocurrency market.

CHAPTER SIX

Advanced Topics in Cryptocurrency

Cryptocurrency and blockchain technology are rapidly changing fields with many advanced concepts and innovations. This chapter explores complex and forward-thinking aspects of the cryptocurrency world, including mining, smart contracts, decentralized applications (DApps), and emerging trends and technologies.

Mining and Proof-of-Work

How Mining Works

Mining is the process that creates new cryptocurrency coins and verifies transactions for the blockchain. In a proof-of-work (PoW) system, miners compete to solve difficult mathematical problems using computational power. The first miner to solve the problem can add a new block of transactions to the blockchain and is rewarded with new coins and transaction fees.

The problem involves finding a nonce (a random number) that, when combined with the block data and hashed, produces a hash value meeting specific criteria (usually a certain number of leading zeros). This process is very resource-intensive, requiring significant energy and specialized hardware.

For example, Bitcoin miners use specialized hardware called ASICs (Application-Specific Integrated Circuits) to perform millions of hash calculations per second to find the correct nonce. Once a block is mined, it is added to the Bitcoin blockchain, and the miner receives newly created bitcoins as a reward.

Environmental Impact and Alternatives (Proof-of-Stake)

The PoW method, while secure and decentralized, consumes a lot of energy, often from non-renewable sources, contributing to a significant carbon footprint. Bitcoin mining, in particular, has been criticized for its environmental impact.

To address these concerns, alternative consensus mechanisms like proof-of-stake (PoS) have been developed. In a PoS system, validators are chosen to create new blocks and validate transactions based on the number of coins they hold and "stake" as collateral. This method greatly reduces energy consumption and computational power needs.

Ethereum, the second-largest cryptocurrency, is moving from PoW to PoS with its Ethereum 2.0 upgrade, aiming to reduce its energy use significantly while maintaining security and decentralization.

Smart Contracts and DApps

How Smart Contracts Work

Smart contracts are self-executing contracts with terms directly written into code. They run on blockchain networks like Ethereum and automatically enforce and execute the terms when certain conditions are met. Smart contracts reduce the need for intermediaries, lower transaction costs, and increase efficiency and transparency.

For instance, a smart contract for a crowdfunding campaign might be programmed to release funds to the project creator only if a certain amount of money is raised by a specific deadline. If the goal isn't met, the funds are automatically returned to contributors, ensuring all parties follow the agreed terms without needing a trusted third party.

Examples of Decentralized Applications

DApps run on blockchain networks and use smart contracts. They cover various use cases, including finance, gaming, social media, and supply chain management.

Some notable DApps include:

Uniswap: A decentralized exchange (DEX) allowing users to trade cryptocurrencies directly from their wallets without a central authority. It uses smart contracts for liquidity pools and automated market making.

Aave: A decentralized lending platform where users can lend and borrow cryptocurrencies. It uses smart contracts to manage loan terms, collateral, and interest rates.

CryptoKitties: A blockchain-based game where players can buy, sell, and breed unique virtual cats, represented by non-fungible tokens (NFTs) on the Ethereum blockchain, showcasing blockchain technology's potential in digital collectibles and gaming.

Future Trends

Scalability Solutions (e.g., Lightning Network, Sharding) Scalability is a major challenge for blockchain networks, as increasing transactions per second without compromising security and decentralization is complex. Some solutions include:

Lightning Network: A layer-2 scaling solution for Bitcoin that enables fast, low-cost transactions by creating off-chain payment channels between users. Transactions within these channels are instant and only settled on the main blockchain when the channel is closed, reducing the main network's load.

Sharding: This technique improves scalability by dividing the blockchain into smaller, parallel chains called shards. Each shard processes a subset of transactions independently, increasing overall network throughput. Ethereum 2.0 is implementing sharding to enhance scalability and performance.

Emerging Technologies and Innovations

The cryptocurrency and blockchain space is continuously evolving, with new technologies and innovations regularly emerging. Notable trends include:

Interoperability: Projects like Polkadot and Cosmos aim to enable different blockchain networks to communicate and interact, creating a more connected blockchain ecosystem.

Decentralized Finance (DeFi): DeFi includes a broad range of financial services built on blockchain networks, such as lending, borrowing, trading, and insurance, aiming to create an open, accessible financial system.

Non-Fungible Tokens (NFTs): NFTs are unique digital assets representing ownership of specific items like art, music, or virtual real estate. They are gaining attention for their potential to revolutionize digital ownership and intellectual property rights.

Blockchain Governance: Decentralized autonomous organizations (DAOs) and on-chain governance mechanisms are being developed to allow blockchain communities to make collective decisions about protocol upgrades, resource allocation, and other important matters. advanced topics in cryptocurrency include a wide range of concepts and technologies shaping the future of digital finance and blockchain innovation.

From mining and consensus mechanisms to smart contracts, DApps, and emerging trends, these topics highlight the potential of cryptocurrencies to transform industries and create new opportunities for decentralized applications and services. Understanding these concepts is essential for staying informed and engaged in the rapidly evolving world of cryptocurrency and blockchain technology.

CHAPTER SEVEN

Case Studies and Real-World Examples

Examining case studies and real-world examples helps us understand how blockchain technology and cryptocurrencies are being used in different sectors. These examples show the practical benefits, challenges, and lessons learned from using these technologies. In this chapter, we will look at successful uses of blockchain and cryptocurrencies in businesses and industries, as well as insights gained from both successes and failures.

Businesses and Industries Using Blockchain

Many businesses and industries have adopted blockchain technology to enhance transparency, security, and efficiency. Here are some key examples:

Supply Chain Management: Companies like IBM and Walmart use blockchain to improve supply chain transparency and traceability. For example, IBM's Food Trust blockchain network helps track the journey of food products from farm to table, enhancing food safety and reducing fraud.

Healthcare: Blockchain is used to secure and streamline medical records. The MediLedger Project is a blockchain-based network designed to improve the pharmaceutical supply chain by ensuring drug authenticity and traceability, combating counterfeit medications.

Finance: Financial institutions use blockchain for cross-border payments and trade finance. Ripple's technology is used by banks like Santander and Standard Chartered to make international transactions faster and cheaper. Platforms like Marco Polo use blockchain to digitize trade finance processes, reducing paperwork and increasing efficiency.

Energy: Blockchain enables peer-to-peer energy trading and better grid management. Power Ledger, an Australian company, has developed a blockchain-based platform that allows consumers to trade excess solar energy directly with each other, promoting renewable energy use and reducing dependency on traditional energy suppliers.

Real-World Use Cases of Cryptocurrencies

Cryptocurrencies are being used in various real-world applications, showing their utility beyond speculative investments:

Remittances: Cryptocurrencies like Bitcoin and Stellar facilitate low-cost, fast remittances. Companies such as BitPesa in Africa and Coins.ph in the Philippines use cryptocurrencies to provide affordable cross-border payment services, bypassing traditional financial intermediaries.

E-commerce: Major online retailers and platforms accept cryptocurrencies as payment. Overstock.com and Shopify merchants, for example, accept Bitcoin and other cryptocurrencies, offering customers more payment options.

Gaming and Virtual Goods: Cryptocurrencies and blockchain technology are transforming the gaming industry by enabling secure in-game purchases and the ownership of virtual goods. Platforms like Enjin allow gamers to create, manage, and trade virtual items using blockchain, ensuring verifiable ownership and scarcity.

Charity and Donations: Cryptocurrencies facilitate transparent and efficient charitable donations. The UN's World Food Programme (WFP) uses blockchain to distribute aid in refugee camps, ensuring funds reach the intended recipients and reducing administrative costs.

Insights from Major Successes

Successful blockchain and cryptocurrency implementations offer valuable insights:

Transparency and Trust: Blockchain's ability to provide immutable, transparent records is a key advantage in industries like supply chain management and healthcare. By ensuring data integrity and traceability, blockchain builds trust among stakeholders and enhances operational efficiency.

Cost Reduction and Efficiency: Blockchain technology can streamline processes, reduce administrative costs, and eliminate intermediaries. This is especially evident in finance and trade, where blockchain solutions have significantly improved transaction speeds and reduced fees.

Increased Security: The decentralized nature of blockchain and its cryptographic security measures protect against data tampering and cyberattacks. This is beneficial in sectors like energy and healthcare, where data security is crucial.

Insights from Failures in the Crypto Space

The cryptocurrency space has also seen notable failures that provide important lessons:

Mt. Gox: The collapse of Mt. Gox exchange in 2014, resulting in the loss of approximately 850,000 bitcoins, highlighted the importance of security and regulatory oversight. It underscored the need for robust security measures, regular audits, and transparent operations in cryptocurrency exchanges.

Bitconnect: Bitconnect, a cryptocurrency lending platform, was exposed as a Ponzi scheme and shut down in 2018. This case emphasized the need for due diligence and skepticism towards investment opportunities that promise unrealistic returns. It also highlighted the importance of regulatory frameworks to protect investors from fraudulent schemes.

DAO Hack: The Decentralized Autonomous Organization (DAO) hack in 2016, where attackers exploited a vulnerability to siphon off $60 million worth of Ether, demonstrated the risks associated with smart contract vulnerabilities. It emphasized the need for thorough code audits, security testing, and the importance of governance structures in managing decentralized projects.

Case studies and real-world examples illustrate the transformative potential of blockchain technology and cryptocurrencies across various industries. By examining both successful implementations and notable failures, we can glean valuable insights into the best practices, challenges, and future directions of this evolving field. Understanding these examples helps to contextualize the practical applications of blockchain and cryptocurrencies and provides a roadmap for navigating the complexities of this dynamic landscape.

CHAPTER SEVEN

Resources and Further Reading

In the ever-changing realm of cryptocurrency and blockchain technology, it is crucial to stay informed and keep up with the latest developments. There are numerous resources available for individuals seeking to expand their knowledge, stay updated on trends, and connect with the wider crypto community. This section presents a brief overview of valuable books, online sources, and community networking opportunities to support your ongoing learning journey.

Recommended Books and Publications

Books provide an excellent avenue for gaining comprehensive knowledge about various aspects of cryptocurrency and blockchain technology. Here are some essential reads:

1. **"Mastering Bitcoin"** by Andreas M. Antonopoulos: This comprehensive guide delves into the technical foundations of Bitcoin and blockchain technology, catering to both beginners and experienced developers.

2. **"Blockchain Basics:** A Non-Technical Introduction in 25 Steps" by Daniel Drescher: This book simplifies the concepts of blockchain in a non-technical manner, making it ideal for individuals new to the subject.

3. **"The Bitcoin Standard:** The Decentralized Alternative to Central Banking" by Saifedean Ammous: This publication explores the economic and historical implications of Bitcoin as a reliable form of money, offering insights into its potential impact on the global financial system.

4. **"Cryptoassets:** The Innovative Investor's Guide to Bitcoin and Beyond" by Chris Burniske and Jack Tatar: This book provides investment strategies and analyses of various cryptoassets, aiding readers in understanding the broader crypto market.

5. **"Blockchain Revolution: How the Technology Behind Bitcoin and Other Cryptocurrencies is Changing the World"** by Don Tapscott and Alex Tapscott: This book explores the transformative potential of blockchain technology across multiple industries.

Online Resources

The internet provides a wide array of resources to keep you informed and updated on the latest happenings in the cryptocurrency field. Here are some valuable online resources:

News Websites:

1. **CoinDesk:** A leading news website that covers all aspects of the cryptocurrency and blockchain industry.

2. **CoinTelegraph:** Another prominent news source that offers the latest updates, analysis, and insights into the world of crypto.

3. Decrypt: Focuses on breaking news, original stories, and investigative reports on cryptocurrencies and blockchain technology.

Educational Platforms:

1. Coursera and Udemy: These platforms offer a variety of courses on blockchain technology and cryptocurrencies, catering to different levels of expertise from beginners to advanced learners.

2. Khan Academy: Provides free educational videos on the fundamentals of Bitcoin and cryptocurrencies.

3. MIT OpenCourseWare: Offers courses and lectures on blockchain technology and its practical applications.

Forums and Discussion Platforms:

1. Reddit: Subreddits like r/Bitcoin, r/Ethereum, and r/CryptoCurrency are vibrant communities where users engage in discussions about news, trends, and technical aspects of cryptocurrencies.

2. BitcoinTalk: One of the oldest forums dedicated to Bitcoin and cryptocurrencies, where you can find discussions covering a wide range of topics.

3. Stack Exchange: A Q&A platform where users can ask technical questions and receive answers from experts in the field.

Communities and Networking

Getting involved with the cryptocurrency community can offer valuable insights, networking chances, and support. By joining online forums, attending meetups, and following influential individuals, you can enhance your knowledge and stay connected with the latest trends and advancements.

Engaging with Crypto Communities and Meetups

Taking part in crypto communities and meetups enables you to connect with like-minded people, exchange knowledge, and stay updated on the latest developments. Here are some ways to get involved:

1. Meetup.com: Look for cryptocurrency and blockchain meetups in your locality. These events often feature speakers, workshops, and opportunities to network.

2. Crypto Conferences and Events: Attend major conferences like Consensus, Bitcoin Conference, and Devcon to hear from industry leaders, participate in panel discussions, and network with professionals.

3. Telegram and Discord Groups: Many cryptocurrency projects and communities have active groups on Telegram and Discord where you can engage in real-time discussions and stay informed about project updates.

Influential Figures and Thought Leaders

Following influential figures and thought leaders in the cryptocurrency space can provide valuable insights and keep you informed about the latest trends and innovations. Here are some notable individuals to follow:

1. Andreas M. Antonopoulos: A well-known Bitcoin advocate and educator, Andreas regularly shares his insights through books, lectures, and social media.

2. Vitalik Buterin: Co-founder of Ethereum, Vitalik frequently shares his thoughts on blockchain technology and its potential applications.

3. Naval Ravikant: An angel investor and entrepreneur, Naval offers deep insights into the broader implications of cryptocurrencies and decentralized technologies.

4. Laura Shin: A journalist and host of the Unchained podcast, Laura covers a wide range of topics related to cryptocurrencies and blockchain technology.

5. Anthony Pompliano: Co-founder of Morgan Creek Digital, Anthony is a prominent figure in the crypto community, known for his podcasts and social media presence discussing Bitcoin and investing.

The realm of cryptocurrency and blockchain technology is vast and ever-evolving. By utilizing books, online resources, and community networking opportunities, you can stay informed and deepen your understanding of this transformative field.

Whether you are a novice or an experienced enthusiast, continuous learning and engagement with the community are crucial in navigating the complexities and staying ahead in the dynamic landscape of cryptocurrencies.

CONCLUSION

As we conclude our exploration of the cryptocurrency realm, it is important to summarize the key points discussed in this book. We began by introducing the fundamental concepts of cryptocurrency, tracing its history and evolution from traditional money to digital currencies.

We delved into the intricacies of blockchain technology, the foundation of cryptocurrency, and examined the mechanics of major cryptocurrencies like Bitcoin and Ethereum. Additionally, we explored practical aspects such as acquiring, storing, and using cryptocurrencies, highlighting both the opportunities and risks involved.

We also covered security measures, common scams, advanced topics like mining and smart contracts, and real-world case studies that demonstrated successful implementations and valuable lessons.

The future of cryptocurrency holds great potential and promise. As blockchain technology matures, it has the potential to disrupt various industries by offering more secure, transparent, and efficient solutions.

Cryptocurrencies are increasingly being integrated into mainstream financial systems, gaining acceptance from businesses, governments, and individuals worldwide. Innovations such as decentralized finance (DeFi), non-fungible tokens (NFTs), and cross-chain interoperability are expanding the possibilities of what cryptocurrencies can achieve, paving the way for new business models and applications.

Predictions and expectations for the cryptocurrency space are diverse and dynamic. Many experts envision a future where digital currencies play a central role in global finance, potentially even replacing traditional fiat currencies.

Advances in blockchain technology are expected to address current challenges such as scalability, security, and interoperability, making cryptocurrencies more accessible and user-friendly. Regulatory developments will continue to shape the landscape, finding a balance between innovation, consumer protection, and financial stability.

As institutional adoption grows, cryptocurrencies may become a standard component of investment portfolios, further legitimizing and stabilizing the market.

In light of these predictions, it is crucial for individuals and businesses to stay well-informed and adaptable. The rapid pace of change in the cryptocurrency world demands continuous learning and vigilance.

Whether you are an investor, a developer, or simply an intrigued observer, understanding the underlying principles and staying up-to-date with the latest trends will be crucial in navigating this complex and exciting domain. Embracing the potential of cryptocurrencies while being mindful of the risks will enable you to make informed decisions and capitalize on the opportunities that arise.

In closing, the rise of cryptocurrencies signifies a paradigm shift in our perception and interaction with money and technology. It challenges traditional financial systems and introduces new possibilities for decentralization, democratization, and innovation.

While the journey of cryptocurrencies is still unfolding, their impact is undeniable, and their future appears promising. As we move forward, it is our collective responsibility to harness the power of these technologies for the greater good, fostering an inclusive, transparent, and resilient financial ecosystem.

"Cryptocurrency for Beginners" helps to equip you with the foundational knowledge and insights needed to navigate the captivating world of digital currencies. As you continue to explore and engage with this evolving field, remember that the true power of cryptocurrency lies not only in its technological advancements but also in its potential to transform lives and societies. Stay curious, stay informed, and most importantly, remain optimistic about the possibilities that the future holds.

Appendix A: Glossary of Terms

Here is a glossary of terms related to blockchain and cryptocurrency:

Blockchain: A decentralized digital ledger that records transactions across multiple computers. It ensures that the record cannot be changed retroactively and consists of blocks linked together.

Cryptocurrency: A digital or virtual currency that uses cryptography for security. It operates independently of a central authority and examples include Bitcoin, Ethereum, and Litecoin.

Wallet: A digital tool for storing and managing cryptocurrency holdings. It can be software-based (hot wallets) or hardware-based (cold wallets).

Exchange: A platform where users can buy, sell, and trade cryptocurrencies. Popular examples include Bybit, Binance, and Coinbase.

Mining: The process of verifying and adding transactions to the blockchain ledger. Miners use powerful computers to solve complex mathematical problems and are rewarded with cryptocurrency.

Decentralization: The distribution of authority, information, and functions across a network instead of being controlled by a single central entity. It is a fundamental principle of blockchain and cryptocurrency.

Smart Contract: A self-executing contract with terms written directly into code. Smart contracts automatically execute and enforce terms without intermediaries.

Token: A digital asset created and managed on a blockchain. Tokens can represent various assets such as utility tokens, security tokens, and stablecoins.

ICO (Initial Coin Offering): A fundraising method where new cryptocurrencies sell a portion of their tokens to early investors in exchange for capital.

DeFi (Decentralized Finance): A movement aimed at creating decentralized financial systems and services using blockchain technology, eliminating the need for traditional intermediaries like banks.

Appendix B: Frequently Asked Questions (FAQ)

Q1: What is cryptocurrency?
A: Cryptocurrency is a digital or virtual currency that uses cryptography for security and operates on decentralized networks based on blockchain technology.

Q2: How do I buy cryptocurrency?
A: To buy cryptocurrency, you need to create an account on a cryptocurrency exchange like Bybit, Binance, or Coinbase. Complete the necessary verification steps, deposit funds, and then place an order to buy the desired cryptocurrency.

Q3: What is a blockchain?
A: A blockchain is a distributed digital ledger that records transactions in a secure, transparent, and immutable manner. Each block contains a set of transactions and is linked to the previous block, forming a chain.

Q4: Is cryptocurrency legal?
A: The legality of cryptocurrency varies by country. In some countries, cryptocurrencies are fully legal and regulated, while in others, they are restricted or banned. It is important to check the local regulations in your country.

Q5: What is a wallet?
A: A cryptocurrency wallet is a digital tool that allows you to store, manage, and transact with your cryptocurrencies. Wallets can be software-based (hot wallets) or hardware-based (cold wallets).

Q6: What are the risks associated with cryptocurrency?
A: Cryptocurrency investments are subject to various risks, including market volatility, regulatory changes, security breaches, and loss of private keys. It is important to conduct thorough research and invest responsibly.

Q7: How are cryptocurrencies taxed?
A: Cryptocurrency taxation varies by jurisdiction. In many countries, cryptocurrencies are treated as property and subject to capital gains tax. It is advisable to

consult with a tax professional to understand the tax implications in your country.

Q8: Can I use cryptocurrency for everyday purchases?

A: While the acceptance of cryptocurrencies for everyday purchases is growing, it is still not as widespread as traditional currencies. Some merchants and online platforms accept cryptocurrencies, but their use in everyday transactions remains limited.

Appendix C: Useful Tools and Software

Here are some useful tools and software for navigating the world of cryptocurrency:

Exchanges: Bybit, Binance, Coinbase, and Kraken are reputable exchanges offering various cryptocurrencies and trading pairs.

Portfolio Trackers: CoinTracking, Delta, and Blockfolio are popular tools that help users track their cryptocurrency investments and monitor market trends.

Analytical Tools: CoinMarketCap, Glassnode, and TradingView provide detailed information, analytics, and charting tools for analyzing cryptocurrencies and market conditions.

These resources can assist beginners in securing their assets, making informed investment decisions, and staying up to date with the cryptocurrency market.

www.ingramcontent.com/pod-product-compliance
Lightning Source LLC
Chambersburg PA
CBHW071950210526
45479CB00003B/878